"I found this book to be some of the best writing I have ever seen on grief, and it is because it is told with the help of a grandson. The concept of grief as a journey—with ups and downs—is very real, as is the concept of learning and growing through our experiences, including grief. We are changed forever by our experiences, and how true it is that we heal but are not cured after losing someone we love.

"The grief of children, if we are open to it and respect it, can help us learn a great deal. As I read the book, I was especially touched by how the author wove in the stories and needs of a child to explain our adult responses to loss.

"It's important to talk about grief in other aspects of life, such as loss of a job, loss of a limb, loss of a marriage, etc. We can't get through life without losses of some kind. It is what we do with the losses—whether we allow them to destroy us or grow through them —that counts most. This book can help lead the way."

Susan T. Hessel
Author, Personal Historian,
Owner: Lessons from Life
and someone who has lived through
and learned from the loss of a child
La Crosse, Wisconsin

"What a fabulous book! As an adoptee who has found loss difficult to deal with, I found *How We Grieve* a resource I wish I'd had many years ago. The personal stories are intricately woven with psychological theory, creating a compassionate, integrated volume to be studied, pondered, and absorbed. I found myself marking almost every page."

Lissa Ann Forbes,
Owner: The Elemental Press
Author of Write from the Inside: Dig for
Treasures, Discover Yourself, Leave a Legacy
Lafayette, Colorado

"This beautifully written book is one of the best books on the stages of grief that I have read! I especially like the fact that its style and simplicity make it ideal for the reader in the midst of the grief process. It flows interestingly and developmentally through the stages developed by Elizabeth Kubler-Ross and Erik Erikson in a way that is understandable to all. The real-life stories and experiences of the author's family members demonstrate the stages of grief realistically in a way that all will be able to identify with.

"I was able to relate to this book both from personal experience, as well as from my twenty years as a counselor in private practice. I only wish it had been available to me then as a bibliotherapy resource to share with my clients. It would have been very helpful and well received. I recommend that current therapists add it to their resource shelf.

"The book is also an excellent journaling guide for clients and friends to work through, as the author has created powerful and insightful questions at the end of each chapter to guide the reader toward self-discovery, self-acceptance, and healing. It also emphasizes and encourages the importance of each of us writing an 'epilogue to our own story.' Halt believes it 'enhances our creativity in shaping our own stories; in finding harmony and balance with our past; and accepting our new place and position in our ongoing life.' I recommend this book very highly."

Eileen Kent
MS Counseling, MS Education
Personal Historian
Owner/Director: Stories of a Lifetime
Utica, New York

"In my personal and professional experience, individuals who are actively grieving need books that are informative, easy-to-read, and heartfelt. *How We Grieve* embraces all of these requirements. The format will appeal to both the general public and professionals working with parents of young children who are dealing with loss.

"As a certified journal writing instructor, I found the exercises at the end of each chapter extremely helpful in providing further opportunity for self-exploration. I intend to use segments of *How We Grieve* in upcoming grief groups."

Rae Hight
RN, MA, LMHC

"In *How We Grieve* Ms. Halt observes the grief expressed by a three-year-old, his parents, and grandparents and relates it to the psychological developmental stages delineated by Erik Erikson and Elizabeth Kubler-Ross. She teaches those who grieve how to build bridges from great loss into a renewed and enriched wholeness that enables them to move forward.

"This book explains the needs of a grieving person in a way that enables friends and loved ones to provide practical help and support during the trauma and process of grief. I heartily recommend this book not only to those experiencing grief, but also to those who want to help others through it.

"This small book distills Pickens Halt's years of personal experience and acquired wisdom as a grief counselor to help those who grieve."

Reverend John Martin
Church of the Foothills
United Church of Christ
Ventura, California

How We Grieve

To Alice—
A friend and
a sister in christ
with love,
Pichaw

How We Grieve

REGRESSION AND REGROWTH

Pickens Halt

CHOOSE YOUR WORDS
Ventura, CA 93003
www.chooseyourwords.net

First Printing, 2007
10 9 8 7 6 5 4 3 2 1

Library of Congress Control Number 2007908175
ISBN 978-0-9797204-0-6

To
Allison Bethany
and her brothers before her,
Thomas Joseph ("T.J.") and
Dustin Michael

CONTENTS

PREFACE

The older I grow and the more of life I experience, the more I become aware that we all revert quickly to a childlike way of being and feeling in the face of trauma. The type, circumstance, or situation of that trauma does not matter. Our response is usually a sudden regression to the small child within each of us. We want and need someone to comfort and console us, and above all, take care of us and make our world right again.

Even though this reaction happens in various traumatic settings, this book will focus on the trauma experienced when someone dear and special in our lives dies and leaves us with a grief that is uniquely ours. My thoughts and reflections are aimed at helping you initiate healing through an understanding and acceptance of your own grief.

I am a marriage, family, and child therapist with more than twenty years of experience in grief counseling. For ten years I worked as bereavement care coordinator in a hospital setting; for several years after my retirement I continued to present lectures for the Archdiocese of Los Angeles in its grief ministry training program; and I still conduct grief support groups in our church.

My professional life has given me an academic understanding of the structure and context of the grief process. The many people I counseled have given me empathy for those who grieve.

It has been my personal life that has brought my head's knowledge and heart's feelings together into a living awareness and understanding of this thing we call grief. In a six-year time span, I experienced the deaths of my mother-in-law, my mother, and three of our grandchildren.

It was the death of our third grandchild that led to the desire to write this book. Allison lived just eight and a half hours. Her three-year-old brother, Kevin, gave me insights and encouragement that opened my heart to healing. He became vivid proof of what I had learned academically. Children experience the same emotions of grief as adults, but they do not have the maturity and life experiences to put those emotions in perspective nor the sophistication of adults to mask or hide those emotions even from themselves.

This book will

- examine grief responses through the actions of a child,
- explore the commonality of grief in children and adults,
- explain grief through regression in Erikson's stages of personality development,
- encourage expressions of grief,
- enable an acceptance of healing.

To help you allow your own grief to be visited with the understanding and acceptance that initiates healing, I invite you to keep a journal. Writing your thoughts and feelings may be easier and feel safer than sharing them with someone, but even a blank piece of paper may feel intimidating. I am including some questions and guidelines at the end of each chapter to give you encouragement. As you journal, know that what you write will be for your eyes only, unless you choose otherwise. Don't edit as you write. Just let the thoughts and feelings flow, paying no attention to grammar, spelling, punctuation, or penmanship. After you read each chapter, pick up your pen and begin.

RECOGNITION

My recognition of those who made this book possible would not be complete without my thanks to

Libby Atwater, my editor and publisher, whose knowledge and patient encouragement helped me bring the manuscript to a publication-ready document,

Catherine Baker, my graphic designer, whose ability and attention to detail made formatting this manuscript a positive experience,

Sylvia Sailer, my friend, whose talent and insight transformed my ideas into a cover for this book,

Bill Frank, whose understanding of the publishing world challenged me to become market ready,

and most especially Anne Lowenkopf and my Thursday morning writing class, for without their guidance and ability to listen, these words would not have found their way to paper.

ACKNOWLEDGMENTS

This book is not a product of my own creation but an outgrowth of the lived experiences of

Tom, our son-in-law, and Becky, our daughter, who provided the foundation that allowed Kevin to express his thoughts and feelings so he could grow through his grief, even as they nurtured each other in their own grief. This really is their story, for it is their children who are our grandchildren.

Ronnie, my husband, who has always been the support I have needed for my own growth.

Peter and Michael, our sons, whose actions and responses to their sister have assured us our family is strong and secure.

Our many friends who have supported us, listened to us, and have been a positive presence in all aspects of our lives, but especially as we journeyed through grief.

Our extended family who are so much a part of who we are.

CHAPTER ONE

"Uncle Peter, look at me!"

Slamming the Door on Bad News

So many exciting things were happening in our family that summer. Each day seemed to hold a sense of anticipation and excitement. Our youngest son, Michael, had just earned his teaching credential, signed a contract at a school not too far from us, and announced his engagement to be married. Our oldest son, Peter, was finding success in his own business and enjoying involvement in political activities and civic organizations. Our middle child and only daughter, Becky, and her husband, Tom, were expecting a new baby—a little brother or sister for their son Kevin. We were a happy family!

In July Tom's company offered him a transfer to their headquarters on the East Coast. This news came as a mixed blessing. Tom's promotion arrived earlier than anticipated and was therefore a welcomed recognition of his skills and abilities. It meant a move to a part of the country Becky had loved since childhood and was thus a dream-come-true for her. It also meant that the new home in Oceanside, California, that had been theirs for barely a year would have to be sold at a time the real estate market was slow. For us it would be the first time we would have our daughter and her family living more than a three-hour drive from us.

Even though the transfer would not take effect until the first of the year, Tom and Becky put their home on the market in hopes of having time to make a profitable sale. The house sold immediately!

Tom's company had an office in Camarillo, not far from our home, where he would be able to work until time for the move to Virginia. We invited Tom, Becky, and Kevin to move in with us for the next several months, and I began to dream of all the ways I could enjoy this soon-to-be new grandchild.

On August 22 Kevin celebrated his third birthday with a family gathering at their home in Oceanside. The next day the process of moving began. Furniture was put into storage until their new home in Virginia would be ready, and we became an expanded family in Ventura.

On Sunday evening of Labor Day weekend, Becky thought the time had come for her to go to the hospital. She and Tom gave goodnight kisses to an excited Kevin and were on their way. It was not long before Tom called from the hospital to say that Becky had been admitted, but the baby's head was not down yet. The doctor thought it would be a long night. Becky sent the message that we were to go to bed. They would call when the birth was imminent.

The next call from Tom was at three o'clock in the morning. Becky had had an emergency Caesarean section, the baby was a girl, and she was on hood oxygen to "pink her up." Becky sent the message that she wanted me to come to the hospital.

When I got to the maternity section, I was met by a nurse carrying a gown for me. As she helped me put it on, she explained that the baby had been having trouble breathing, had been intubated, and was being stabilized so that a transfer team could move her to a nearby hospital with a neonatal intensive care unit.

Before I could react to what I was told, I was ushered into the recovery room where Tom and Becky were anxiously waiting to see little Allison before she would be whisked away to the neighboring hospital. We did not have to use words to communicate the reality of what was happening. We knew all too well that "intubated" meant Allison was on a respirator. This was a nightmare we had lived before.

In rapid succession several events occurred. Tom and I were taken into the hallway to consult with a doctor. We could see the transfer team huddled around Allison in such a tight circle that we could barely glimpse the baby who was the focus of everyone's attention. The decision was made that Allison was too fragile to risk passing by Becky's bed on the way to a better-equipped environment, and this much-anticipated newborn was suddenly on her way to a different hospital.

Becky developed chills and an elevated temperature, so I stayed with her and Tom followed Allison. Somewhere in the midst of all this activity I found a phone and called Ronnie and then Peter. Peter immediately left his home in Los Angeles to come to Ventura to be with Kevin so Ronnie could join me at the hospital.

At 10:24 Labor Day morning Allison died. We all felt as though we were in a time warp. We made the decision that Tom would be the one to tell Kevin of the birth and death of his little sister. Ronnie and I returned home to find Uncle Peter and Kevin involved in the normal events of a day in the life of a three-year-old.

It was not long before Tom arrived. Ronnie, Peter, and I went to the master bedroom to give Tom and Kevin time alone in the living room. We could hear Tom gently telling Kevin that his Mom was okay. His little sister, Allison, had been born; she had been very sick, and she had died.

Immediately Kevin ran down the hall into the bedroom with us, slammed the door behind him, climbed on the bed, and began wildly bouncing with his arms flung out, yelling, "Uncle Peter, Uncle Peter! Look at me!"

The door opened, Tom quietly stepped inside, Kevin collapsed into his Dad's open arms, and they both cried.

Kevin was barely three years old. A child too young, some would say, to know grief. In reality, Kevin knew very well what he was feeling and experiencing. What he lacked was adult sophistication and maturity to try to control or hide his emotions.

How many of us, when we hear bad news, want to slam the door on what we have just heard? To run from the news that we wish we could shut away? To draw attention to ourselves, so we can control what is happening around us? Kevin, in his innocence, did what he felt he needed to do. He put his innate desires into action until, in his Dad's protective arms, he could allow himself to cry. Over the following days and weeks Kevin continued to show me the truth of the words "and a little child shall lead them."

Erik Erikson in his theory of personality development lays out the stages of our growth from birth to the end of life[1]. He states that each stage is a struggle between two characteristics. Our resolution of each struggle helps us to develop a quality we need for a healthy adaptation to life.

Erikson's theory contains eight stages. These stages begin with our first year of life and end with a maturity that is not defined by age. That initial struggle in our infancy, he says, is between trust and mistrust to develop the quality of hope. The final struggle in his theory is between integrity and despair in order to develop the quality of wisdom.

---

1   See Erikson's chart in the Appendix.

My theory is that we may be a mature person developing a sense of integrity and growing in wisdom from life's experiences, but when death claims a loved one, we quickly revert to the initial stage of our life. Despite our age, we are once again involved in the struggle of trust against mistrust with the need to find a basis for hope. We become childlike in our needs and want someone to take us in a protective embrace and make the hurt go away. We are encased in an adult body that proclaims outwardly that we are capable and able; we must cope even as we protest the reality of what has happened.

On that day in early September, Kevin immediately became a grief-filled child when he heard that his baby sister had died. On a basic level he knew something had happened that was beyond his control, and at the same time he felt a sudden surge of many emotions. Most likely those initial emotions were feelings of hurt, disappointment, fear, anger, and an overwhelming sense of loss. A three-year-old could deal with any one of those feelings by collapsing in tears, but when they came as a complete package it was too much. Kevin's world had fallen apart and he now had two choices: he could collapse immediately, or he could attempt to be in control and restore his world to its rightful balance. Intuitively he acted to recreate his world, but reality coupled with protection followed him in the guise of his dad, and he collapsed in tears.

In the adult world, we have the same choices. If we choose collapse, those around us immediately become concerned that we are "falling apart" or are "unable to cope." As a result, many of us feel a need to take on protective armor, to hide our feelings, and thus shield others from concern for us. By doing this we earn an honorary title—"being strong"—but that armor and title may become stumbling blocks to our need to mourn. It's our adult sophistication that makes us so markedly different from a little child.

Most often, though, we try to slam the door on bad news and keep our world in its "rightful" orbit. We usually don't act out this desire as graphically as Kevin did. Our bodies take over in an effort to protect ourselves; we operate on automatic pilot. We are in a state of shock. If the reality of this death and an awareness of all that it will mean to us were immediately experienced, we would be so overwhelmed we would be incapacitated. Others, seeing our shocked state, might say we are in denial. In truth, we are in a state of disbelief.

If we can accept the likelihood that we quickly revert to childlike ways of being and feeling in a time of grief, perhaps we can begin to give voice to our needs and be a bit more gentle with ourselves and honest with our emotions. By doing so, we allow the protection and soothing we so desperately need to happen.

QUESTIONS

1. Was there a time when you, like Kevin, felt a
    need to slam the door on bad news?

2. If you did not actually slam the door, what did
    you do?

3. Can you identify a person who, like Kevin's dad,
    enabled you to cry? Or was there no one?

4. Reflecting on that time, write your remembrance,
    your thoughts and feelings. Write whatever
    comes to mind, and write until the thoughts
    stop.

CHAPTER TWO

"Dying makes me sad."

Growing Through Grief

Kevin was two-and-a-half years old when he received the video, *The Land Before Time*, as a Christmas gift. Its story is about a couple of orphaned baby dinosaurs searching for the green valley where they will find the nourishment they need to survive.

A few weeks after Christmas, Kevin was visiting us. He, Becky, and I were seated at the dining room table having an afternoon "coffee break." Becky and I were chatting about something superficial, when Kevin, with a faraway look in his eyes, made a quiet statement: "Dying makes me sad."

We were caught by surprise to hear such a profound statement from one so young. We knew we needed to pursue the subject with him, so we agreed with him that dying made us sad also. Kevin then told us that the baby dinosaurs in his video were sad when the mother dinosaur died, and he felt sad when he thought about that.

I believe we, as grieving adults, could benefit greatly if we observed young children and then allowed ourselves to identify our needs and express our own grief as openly as they are able to do. A two-year-old is very much able to be aware of death and the sadness that it brings. There was a time in our lives that we, too, intuitively knew these things, but in our adult sophistication we have suppressed our need to grieve in order to be more compliant with the world in which we live.

The orphaned baby dinosaur in *The Land Before Time* followed a basic instinct that pulses in all of us—a need to find the green valley (where life is fresh and new and thriving again) and the nourishment (not just physical, but emotional and spiritual) needed to survive.

In Charles Schultz's "Peanuts" cartoon strips, Charlie Brown's inept tendencies frequently lead Lucy to show her exasperation by using the exclamation, "Good grief, Charlie Brown!" Taken together, the two words are a familiar expression, but examined as two separate words they seem incongruent when brought together as a phrase.

What could possibly be "good" about "grief"? Aside from their combination to form an expletive of exasperation, can these two words be combined to state a truth? Can there be such a thing as *good* grief?

"Growing through grief" may sound as incongruent as Lucy's expletive. When I worked as a grief counselor in a hospital setting, I conducted support groups for people experiencing grief due to the death of a valued person in their lives. From my own personal experiences and my observations of those who participated in these support groups, I became aware that we do grow in positive ways if we allow ourselves to experience all we need to feel and acknowledge during a time of grief. We can emerge from this period in our lives as better people. We become better in the sense that we are more sensitive to others, more compassionate, more aware of the value and purpose of life, and stronger in our faith. The death of a loved one is a terrible price to pay for personal growth, but we **can** grow during this traumatic time.

What is this traumatic time? What is this thing we call grief? My name tag when I worked as a grief counselor proclaimed me to be a "Bereavement Care Coordinator." My first day on the job taught me that vocabulary would be a part of my job description. The young man in personnel who made my name tag misspelled "bereavement," then while remaking the badge asked me the meaning of the word. Being asked for the definition of my title or an explanation of what I did became a regular occurrence.

What is "bereavement"? "Bereave" comes from an archaic English word "bereafian" meaning "to be stripped of something of value by a force beyond our control." Death is a force we cannot control. Death comes and takes from us a person we value, and we are

11

immediately a bereaved person. All that we feel, all the emotions we experience due to the death of this special person, is what we call "grief." How we work through these feelings and how we express our emotions is what we call "mourning."

Unfortunately, in this modern era, we can be a bereaved person feeling all the emotions and symptoms of grief, but not given the time, space, encouragement, or even permission to mourn.

Due to the advances in medical technology in this country, life expectancy has increased to the point we can be very mature people before we experience the death of someone of great significance in our lives. If we have not gone through a time of grief and mourning, we do not know what to expect when we become a bereaved person. We are ill equipped for this journey through grief.

This journey through grief is a trip none of us seeks. A planned trip usually begins with a desire—a dream or a hope—and progresses to an itinerary and a plan. All too often, though, our journey through grief begins in fear, and we have no map to show us the way. Where are we going? Is there a destination? Why must we take this journey? Must we make this trip alone?

Grief is a solitary journey even though others may travel the same path. Each of us is a unique individual, and we each experience our grief in the context of our own personality and relationships. In that sense, the pain of our grief is ours alone and no other person can bear it for us. Yet even in our differences, we can still experience support and know companionship so that we do not travel in isolation.

What do we need for this journey through grief? We need to take our memories with us, but often our memories seem a burden until we are able to share them with another by telling our story. So we need the listening ears of understanding people: family, friends, or a faith community. We need permission to identify our losses and to speak our loved ones' names.

We need to journey into ourselves for a time of reflection. We need to slow down, be silent, be still, and even in solitude, have some care for the hurt that is ours. And we need to be open to receive and accept satisfying comforts when we encounter them.

After our time of solitude we need encouragement to step out into the path of life again. We need to recognize that traveling on does not mean we no longer miss our loved one, but that we are now able to be aware of the gratitude we hold that this life touched ours and we are a better person for that touch.

Being aware of the potential for growth in a healing journey through grief, I named our hospital grief support groups "Growing Through Grief," and used the analogy of a bare root tree to gain an understanding of the grief process and the hidden potential in this grief work.

If you go to a nursery during the bare root season, you will see racks of bare root shrubs and trees. They look like unidentifiable dead sticks dangling a tag and held together with twine or baling wire. To the untrained eye, the tag is needed for identification of this lifeless-appearing plant as a rose, apple, peach, pear, or plum.

We, as people, may have a kindred feeling toward these bare root specimens. In the early stages of our grief we may feel more dead than alive. Faced with the enormity of the loss we have experienced, we feel we will fall apart if some means is not found to tie us up or wire us together. Many of us feel stripped of our identity without this special person to give us purpose or direction; and so we need that name tag to proclaim who we are to ourselves if not to the outside world. In the midst of our time of grief we feel vulnerable, as though our very roots are exposed, as are the roots on bare rootstock.

Yet, if that bare root plant is placed in the proper environment—planted in fertile soil, given a stake for support, exposed to sunshine and fresh air, watered and fed, the life force that appeared dead begins to flow. Initially it starts in unseen ways, hidden in the root structure that spreads out and grows, giving the plant more stability and a source of nourishment. Gradually that life force surges into the parts of the plant that can be seen. Buds appear and blossom, leaves grow, and in time flowers and fruit appear. What had appeared dead and lifeless becomes vital and productive. In time and with care, bare roots bear fruit.

As grieving people, we, too, need a proper environment. Grief can thrust us into a dormant period of our lives. During this period we need nourishment, shelter, and protection; we need the support and encouragement of friends and loved ones so our life force can begin to flow again. By giving ourselves permission to experience all we need to go through during this time, we can take our journey through grief and emerge strengthened and productive.

QUESTIONS

1. Has there been a time when you were bereaved but not given the time, space, encouragement, or permission to mourn?

2. Has there been a "bare root" season in your life when you felt you had lost your life force and were stripped of all signs of identity?

3. Journal about that bare root time describing the ways you felt stripped of identity and life force. If a tag of identification had been tied to you, what would the label have said?

4. Do you think there is such a thing as "good grief?"

CHAPTER THREE

"Somebody, anybody! I need help!"

Erikson's Stages Reversed

After Allison's death, Kevin found going to bed at night difficult. He had quickly changed from being proud of his three-year-old "big boy" status to making demands more typical of "the terrible twos." Night after night Kevin would call for his mom or dad, pleading for another story, to be rocked again, or to have somebody lie down with him. One night the process was particularly long and tedious. When Tom responded to Kevin's next call, he discovered that Kevin had wet the bed. Tom called Becky to bring some dry sheets.

Then came Kevin's voice, " 'Franmudder!' 'Handdad!' Somebody! Anybody! I need help! I'm all wet!" When I entered the room Kevin was helping strip the bed. He looked up at the room suddenly full of busy adults bumping into each other in their haste to meet his demands and smiled, "You people take good care of me."

What is it that we so desperately need in our time of grief? For Kevin, it was the basic need to know that somebody would take care of him. To him it was simple logic: Allison was sick when she was born. She needed somebody to take care of her. Allison had died, therefore, she had not been receiving the care she needed. This logic left Kevin with a fear that the people he trusted in his life might fail to take care of him. His sense of trust had eroded. He had regressed to that basic struggle of Erikson's first developmental stage: Trust versus Mistrust. It took Kevin many nights of multiple testing before he had the proof he needed that indeed he could once again trust us to care for him.

We can easily see a small child's regression to more infantile behavior during a traumatic time. If we are not too emotionally involved, we can identify a child's needs and attempt to meet them.

As adults we mask our needs behind "appropriate" behavior and wonder why our needs are not met. Before we can accept the soothing and receive the protection as Kevin did, we must identify our needs. One of the basic needs of each of us is to know there is someone who cares.

In the initial phase of our grief we may not be aware of specific needs, but as the shock and disbelief begin to wane, our needs begin to emerge. We experience a rapid reversal and descend into more childlike ways of being. Our problem as mature people is that we have built a persona of wholeness and integrity that serves us adequately. The sophistication of adulthood proclaims we *should* be able to continue to operate as a whole and complete person. Yet in this new world of grief we feel broken and incomplete.

Erikson, as discussed in a previous chapter, identifies the mature stage of our life as being the struggle between integrity (sense of wholeness) and despair. I have observed that in grief, as the reality of loss begins to emerge, we start to despair and then begin that rapid reversal to more childlike ways of being. By reversing, or turning upside down, Erikson's chart, we can see this regression to childlike ways of being.

INTEGRITY   DESPAIR
                 (Wisdom)
GENERATIVITY   SELF-ABSORPTION
                 (Care)
INTIMACY   ISOLATION
                 (Love)
IDENTITY   ROLE CONFUSION
                 (Fidelity)
INDUSTRY   INFERIORITY
               (Competence)
INITIATIVE   GUILT
                 (Purpose)
AUTONOMY   SHAME
                 (Will)
TRUST   MISTRUST
                 (Hope)

My most graphic portrayal of this reversal was an encounter with a middle-aged woman who was widowed after more than thirty years of marriage. She said, "My life with my husband was just what the minister who married us had said, 'The two of you shall be one.' We were one. We were a couple in all that we did. Now that he has died, I am half of nothing." Being "half of nothing" is ultimate despair.

As a wife she had felt a sense of wholeness and integrity in being part of a couple with her husband. Now, as a widow, that sense of **integrity** had quickly given way to **despair**. In this despair she experienced a loss of wholeness that was manifested in a physical need to hold herself together. Almost all of us have felt that need. We lower our head and wrap our arms around our body in an attempt to look inward to ensure we are still intact. We become extremely self absorbed.

In this **self absorption** we no longer have the desire or energy to reach out to others with a helping hand (Erikson's stage of Generativity), so we begin to isolate ourselves. **Isolation** would seem to insulate from the possibility of new grief, but in actuality it guarantees a loss of intimacy with others that becomes a grief in itself.

Isolation also opens the door to **role confusion**. Without intimacy we lose our sense of identity and become very confused about our role in life. My widowed friend would lament, "I used to have a purpose in life. I shopped for his food. I cooked his meals. I knew what he wanted, and I got it for him." And her lamentations led her to a sense of **inferiority**. She was no longer industrious because she did not have her beloved husband with needs that she could meet. She no longer felt competent.

Guilt weighed heavily upon her. Without a purpose for her life she had lost her initiative. Guilt gave way to **shame**. She would wail, "I am so ashamed. I don't seem to be able to do anything. I don't have anyone I can trust, and I can't even trust myself."

Her reversal from integrity to **mistrust** was rapid. This can happen rapidly for any of us during the traumatic time we call grief. With the death of someone dear to us, we suddenly become a bereaved person who feels the need to be comforted as gently as a mother would comfort an infant. We all have a desire for someone to step into our life, wrap their arms around us, and make everything right again.

When we are thrust into a time of grief, this painful regression may happen. Unlike Kevin, we may not be able to cry out in the night for "somebody, anybody," but we can be open to the "somebodies" and "anybodies" who are in our lives. They are the supportive people around us who would like to help but don't know just what to do. They are the people who may be annoying us with their nonspecific offers saying, "Let me know if you need anything." They want to help, but don't know our needs. Kevin was vocal and active in exploring his inventory of needs. As an adult, we attempt to put on a brave face that camouflages our needs, not only from others but also from our very self.

I have vivid childhood memories of summer afternoons spent playing with my doll on my grandmother's front porch. Grandmother had two big rocking chairs on her porch. Often as I played she would rock in one chair and a friend would rock in the other. Sometimes they rocked quietly, sometimes they talked, and it was always comforting to me. I was in the presence of someone who cared about me.

In grief we need the presence of someone who cares, someone who will figuratively rock with us in silence until a sense of companionship develops that allows thoughts and feelings to be put into words. The friend who comes with an agenda to bring cheer or divert our thoughts to more pleasant things is not a rocking companion. Words poured out to fill silence can allow us to hide feelings and needs in superficial conversation. A rocking companion is the friend who listens, rather than talks, giving us the opportunity to express ourselves how and when we have the need.

To be that rocking companion to a spouse, family member, or friend may not be an easy or natural role. For many, the ability to sit quietly with another who is in pain is an acquired skill. Compassion makes us want to take away the hurt rather than be still as pain becomes palatable. Our immediate desire is to speak words of hope or to divert a loved one's thoughts to more pleasant times.

Becoming a rocking companion begins by initially responding to the demands that grief places on the bereaved, as Kevin's parents did to his pleas to be rocked or have one more story. An understanding of grief can be the tool needed to move beyond an immediate response and allow us to become a rocking companion.

Grief is not resolved by avoidance. It needs to be explored and experienced. We come to healing not by going around or under this thing called grief, but by going through it. Grief work is just that—it is work, hard work. And the work of grief is not completed in isolation, but in an atmosphere of support from one who cares, from one who can be trusted to rock with us companionably. It is a trial-and-error process for both the bereaved and the one who cares.

In my role as a grief counselor I have spent much time just sitting with someone who was feeling lost and alone. As a sense of togetherness began to develop, words began to flow, and then memories took form and were shared. As I listened, I often became aware of an inner calm arising from the one who finally allowed his or her thoughts and feelings to emerge and be identified. This calm reminds me of the comfort that strengthened me as a child, and I am aware that it is based on the reality that someone cares enough to be present and to listen. In that atmosphere, mistrust begins to give way once again to trust.

Trust is like a muscle. If it is not exercised, it becomes useless. Kevin cried out in the night, and the supportive parents and grandparents in his life came running. Like Kevin, we adults have that basic need to know that *somebody* cares. We need to exercise our trust and respond to the people around us who care. Each of us needs to trust ourselves enough to put the story of our loss into words and allow hope to begin to take root. Erikson said, "It is never too late to go back and do a better job."

QUESTIONS

1. What needs have you masked behind "proper" behavior or a brave face?
   What is it that you want so desperately in your time of grief?

2. Have you felt a loss so profound that you felt a need for someone to step in, put arms around you, and make it all right again?
   Can you identify your steps of regression?

3. Can you name someone who is or could be your "rocking companion," giving you the courage and support to take off your mask?

4. In your journal, begin to trust yourself to put into words your story of loss. Be open to seeing the seeds of hope start to take root.

CHAPTER FOUR

"I think that baby is dying."

Telling Our Story

While Becky was recovering from Allison's delivery, Kevin went to the hospital with us to see his mom. Intrigued by the nursery windows, he ran ahead to climb the two steps to the platform that allowed siblings to view a new brother or sister. Several babies were bundled in either pink or blue blankets, but one little newborn, with ink still on his feet from having his footprints recorded for posterity, was naked under the warming lights. Kevin pointed to that kicking, crying little one and said softly, "I think that baby is dying."

We assured him that baby was not sick and would soon have his feet washed and be wrapped up. Kevin replied, "Then I'll take that baby home with me." Our statement that the baby had a mommy and daddy to take him home caused him to point to each baby in turn and say, "I'll take that one, then." When he learned that each baby had someone to take him or her home,

Kevin stepped down from the platform and said, "My baby died, but I still love her."

Children experience the same emotions of grief as adults but lack maturity and life experiences to put their grief in perspective. It is our adult sophistication that makes our ways of mourning so different from that of children. One of the remarkable things about young children is their ability to acknowledge and express their grief, sometimes with great intensity. They then suddenly take a break from their emotional upheaval by becoming involved in ordinary, even enjoyable, life-renewing activities.

If we can accept the idea that we quickly revert to childlike ways of being and feeling in a time of grief, perhaps we can begin to give voice to our needs and be a bit more gentle with ourselves, allowing the protection and soothing we so desperately need to happen.

When Allison died I found myself split into several different roles. I was not only a grieving grandmother, I was also a protective mother wanting to take away the terrible hurt our daughter was suddenly experiencing. I was a concerned grandmother turned overnight into primary caregiver for Kevin, since his mom was in the hospital and his dad was spending most of his time there as they attempted to deal with their overwhelming loss. I was the professional grief counselor feeling as though I was standing outside of myself watching all this take place, knowing what "should" be done, and feeling powerless to make anything happen.

I would observe Kevin sinking and surfacing in his attempts to address and understand his grief. I knew I needed to give voice to my own sense of loss, but no matter which direction I turned, I faced someone who was filled with his or her own grief and needed comfort and help.

Hearing Kevin express his unending love for Allison gave me an insight to my own need. I poured out my dreams, my heartbreak, and especially my love in a letter to her. It was not an easy task, but it was a step in the direction of healing. Grief is an emotional weight that sits heavily on us. As I wrote, I began to feel this grief's weight lighten. Even though I was not able to complete my letter to Allison at first writing, I was able to get in touch with my own feelings and become aware that my love for Allison was greater than my grief over her death. I began to breathe more easily.

As I cried my way through writing to Allison I was suddenly in touch with yet another role. I was a little girl wanting my mother to soothe me and take away my hurt, but Mother was on the other side of the country and telephone lines could not wrap her arms around me. On an adult level I knew Mother's nursing background would be able to comprehend the medical complexities that were such a struggle to us, so I began another letter telling Mother the details of Allison's brief life.

Telling our story is a crucial step in working our way through grief. We need to be able to tell what has happened over and over again until it becomes an accepted part of our own personal history and of whom we are now. The heartfelt injury we call grief is an assault not only on our emotions but also on our body. It needs to be tended in much the same manner we would tend a physical injury—with gentle and active care.

If we were involved in a serious accident and lost an arm or a leg, we might say we were dismembered, for a part, or member, of our body was now missing. An artificial limb could be made, we would be re-membered and could begin to function adequately again.

When death claims someone dear to us, we often feel as though a part of us has been taken away. We no longer feel whole; we are dismembered. We cannot replace our loved one with another person, but we can begin to let our memories surface as we call to mind all the ways this special person was a part of us. We re-member ourselves, make ourselves whole again, by remembering.

Putting thoughts and feelings into written words began to give me stability. I was caught in that primary struggle Erikson describes of Trust versus Mistrust. As I began to trust myself to tell my story, initially in written form, I began to feel Hope re-enter my life. I became aware of friends who were anxiously attempting to be supportive, and I could now respond to invitations to walk in the park or on the beach. In these activities I could begin to tell my story to a caring listener and re-member myself. I discovered that sometimes a "rocking companion" comes in the guise of a walking companion.

QUESTIONS

1. Write a letter to your loved one who is no longer a physical presence in your life. Tell this special person of your love, your loss, your hurts, your fears.

2. Write to the person you would most want to be your rocking companion, and in your letter tell your story of loss. As you remember and tell your story, journal the ways you experience a sense of reconnecting—of re-membering yourself.

CHAPTER FIVE

"If you'd bring my baby home…"

Magical Thinking

Tom and Kevin developed a ritual of long talks while Kevin took his bath. Tom would sit on the bathroom floor as Kevin played in the tub, and they often had deep philosophical discussions. Kevin did not ask many questions about Allison and her death, but he listened intently to comments, and he made statements. Tom would tell Kevin that mommy and daddy might cry; their tears were not because they were upset with Kevin, but that they were sad that Allison had died.

Kevin told his dad, "If you would bring my baby home, I could give her some soft medicine, and she could get well."

Most young children adapt to major or traumatic changes by asking questions or making statements over and over again until they accept the fact that the answer is not going to change. Kevin attempted to deal with Allison's death by repeating his belief he could restore her. At times he would phrase it differently by saying, "If you had brought my baby home, we could have glued her back together." This belief was his attempt not only to understand this mystery we call death, but to explore all possibilities of his power to right this wrong.

Young children see themselves as the center, or focal point, of all that is happening around them. Their ego-centric view of the universe shows itself in many ways. When Peter, our oldest son, was in third grade, he was excited about the things he was learning in school. He loved to display his newly gained knowledge by asking questions worded in ways that might elicit a wrong answer he could correct. One night, in his eagerness to demonstrate his new knowledge that the sun did not rise, he told us some things he was learning about the solar system. He asked, "Do you know why the sun comes up each morning?"

Three-year-old Michael suddenly sat up straight in his chair, pointed to himself with both hands, and exclaimed, "For me!"

This self-centered view of life can foster the belief in children that if they think something and then it happens, their thoughts made it so. When their thoughts or wishes are realized in a positive way, they feel fulfilled and powerful. But if things go wrong, they may see themselves as doing "wrong" or being "bad." This is a phenomenon of childhood called "magical thinking," and it is demonstrated in many ways. Think of the seriousness and care expressed in acting out the childhood chant, "Step on a crack, break your mother's back." Often, however, we do not see the actions that would indicate a child has taken on the mantle of guilt because he or she perceives that the thought or idea has caused calamity.

I do not believe magical thinking is limited to childhood. As adults, we still cling to an element of this phenomenon, especially when we revert to childlike ways of being during a time of grief. We want so much for things to be "right" in our world, but they are not; therefore, we begin to look for the reason they have gone wrong. All too often we end up pointing a finger of blame at ourselves.

When I was in high school, I spent a week one summer at a church camp on a college campus. My roommate, a girl from another city, was a stranger to me. She was quiet and very withdrawn. None of my attempts to get to know her or to do things with her met with any success.

On our last evening together we gathered to sing songs around a campfire. The fire was dying when someone began singing

"Blest be the tie that binds

Our hearts in Christian love..."

With a loud sob, my roommate jumped to her feet and ran off into the dark. I still can feel the chill and sense of helplessness I experienced later that night when she had been found and told her story.

She said the song had been sung at her brother's funeral, and she had killed her brother. She explained that he had been getting ready to go on a scouting trip and asked to borrow her flashlight. She'd answered, "No, I won't lend it to you because you'll probably lose it." The truck full of other scouts was waiting for him at the curb, and the driver impatiently blew the horn. Her brother grabbed her flashlight and ran out the door saying, "Well, I'm taking it anyway."

She shouted back, "Oh, drop dead!"

When the scouts arrived at camp, the gate was closed. Her brother leapt from the back of the truck to open the gate, lost his balance, fell, and broke his neck. My roommate was convinced that her thoughts and words had caused his death.

It does not take as dramatic an event as this young girl experienced for magical thinking to become part of our perception. We may know in very concrete ways the cause of a loved one's death, but the internal response can still be self-blame—an unspoken sense of "I am the cause." Even knowing that a death did not happen because of our hurtful words or deliberate actions, the guilty feeling can persist.

Over the years I have heard self-blame expressed in various forms. They can be summarized by the lady who told me in great detail on numerous occasions that even though her husband had a history of heart disease, his sudden death had been unexpected. Since his death, his doctor had told her repeatedly that his final heart attack had been so massive that death was instantaneous. The doctor said that nothing she, or anyone else, could have done would have made a difference. Still, one day in repeating her story to me, this widow added a part she had never told previously. She had fixed her husband's lunch and left him to eat it by the pool while she went to the grocery store. When she returned, she had found him dead in his chair with his lunch uneaten. Her added comment, "If I had not gone to the store, he would still be alive today," is a powerful example of magical thinking.

Ironically, as children and adults we can each realize our lack of power, yet we still think we are powerful enough to have made a difference. Release from this burden of blame begins by putting our thoughts into words. Once the words are spoken, the thought is out there, separated from our internal self. Magical thinking begins to lose its grasp and acceptance of reality can come into focus. The safe environment that enables us to voice our "wrong" is another instance of the help and support that can come through a "rocking" companion.

After expressing ourselves, we can experience an almost-instant change, as though hearing our thoughts out loud makes us suddenly aware of the impossibility of our imagined power . There are times, though, when voicing the imagined ability is only the first step toward working through this burden of guilt. Although our words are spoken and the inability to have changed the situation is acknowledged, the guilt lingers. There is still a sense that "I should have done something differently."

Speaking our thoughts takes us outside the mask of adult sophistication that separates us from the spontaneity of little children. It is a step toward working our way back to a sense of integrity in Erikson's stages; finding enough trust to begin to deal with the shame that has arisen from the feeling that not only did I do wrong, perhaps I am wrong. It is how we take the initiative to deal with this thing called guilt.

Guilt is the most insidious of the many emotions we experience in the tumult of grief, for it is usually not guilt in the true meaning of the word. Guilt is a sense of culpability that merits condemnation or blame. It is a needed emotion and a foundational block that helps us live as civilized people. Like all emotions, we need to be careful that we do not label it "good" or "bad," for it is an honest expression of what we are experiencing and is a part of who we are at that moment. For lack of a better term, I call this grief-induced guilt that arises from magical thinking "false guilt."

Whether "true" or "false," guilt needs our attention. We need to be able to work through this emotion and move from feeling responsible to expressing remorse, then to acknowledging regret, and finally working toward resolution. Healthy resolution is that time when we can change "if only" to "now that this has happened, how will I continue to live?" It can be enticing to prefer guilt to the realization we lack power over past events. Resolution demands that we take the initiative to create a growing sense of purpose.

A few weeks after Allison's death, Kevin developed a routine of emphasizing his need for his daily fluoride tablet, making sure it came from the container with his name on it, and ending with his declaration of growing strong and healthy. He was playing an active part in resolving his growing knowledge of the powerlessness of us all to have done anything to keep Allison alive. He needed to feel a sense of control, if not in what had gone wrong in Allison's brief life, then to protect himself. He wanted stability to return to his world, and he was taking an active role to make that happen.

QUESTIONS

1. What do you wish you could have done differently?
   What guilt, spoken or held secret, are you carrying?

2. Is this guilt rooted in magical thinking?
   Be honest with yourself; is your guilt "false" guilt?

3. Journal your thoughts/feelings being open to express remorse or regret rather than responsibility.

4. Take the initiative. Describe at least one step you can make to take care of yourself.

CHAPTER SIX

"I need to write some numbers."

Finding Security

By the next Labor Day weekend, stability had returned to Kevin's world. He and his parents had settled into their new home in Virginia and begun to orient themselves to new friends and activities. Kevin had participated in various preschool activities at a local park. He was proud of his understanding of what constituted an emergency and his newly learned ability to dial 9-1-1. He had celebrated his fourth birthday and was filled with excitement at being a student at Hope Preschool.

Kevin was so enthusiastic about going to school that he began to take great delight in "writing" and developed a habit of carrying a pencil and pad of paper with him when he accompanied his mom on errands. Once, after going to a Chinese restaurant for dinner, he carefully produced row after row of neatly spaced small lines at various angles and of different lengths on his pad of paper. He then announced that he could not read it, but he could write Chinese.

One day he approached Becky with his pad and pencil announcing, "I need to write some telephone numbers."

Becky responded, "Whose number do you need to write?"

Kevin admitted, "I don't know. I need to have some numbers so I can call somebody to come take care of me if you die."

Becky assured him she felt healthy and hoped she would live to see him grow up. She added that even if something happened to her, Dad would be there to take care of him. Kevin replied, "I was thinking about the time you both die."

Becky sat down with Kevin and said, "Dad and I talked about this, and we made a will to protect you in case something happened to both of us. A will is a special paper that names Grandmother and Granddad as the people to take care of you if both of us should die." Kevin listened, then wrote down our phone number and confidently carried his pencil and paper to his room.

Even though stability had returned to Kevin's life, he needed an added sense of security. From experience he had learned that death can be unexpected. He had explored his thoughts and finally come to the realization that he did not have the power to change or reverse this thing called death. In the year since the beginning and end of Allison's short life, time had taught him that death is permanent. He had made great progress in dealing with his grief, showing his emotions, and voicing his concerns. Through repeated testing, he had regained assurance that his parents would take good care of him, but he still had issues that needed to be resolved. Starting preschool brought a new challenge—separation from Mom and Dad. As Kevin's life events pulled him forward, would he be secure?

Insecurity is another obstacle we all face in our journey through grief. We exercise some elements of trust, regain a sense of autonomy, and begin to take the initiative needed to relieve the burden of guilt. Just as stability begins to be tangible, we begin to feel inadequate. Will there be any semblance of security in life? We are in the stage Erikson identifies as Industry versus Inferiority.

A few years ago on a trip to England and Scotland I was fascinated with the abundance of old castles and cathedrals. Time after time tour guides pointed to the construction of the arches that formed the windows and doors of these ancient stone structures. Pointing to the wedge-shaped stone at the summit of an arch, the guide emphasized that all the building's pieces were held together by this all-important keystone. Security may well be the keystone we need as we continue to reconstruct ourselves in grief.

Often we feel divided as we journey through grief as though we have a foot in two camps. One is the past and all that we remember in our connection with our loved one. The other is the future and its imagined uncertainties without our loved one by our side. A sense of security acts as the bridge to connect the past and the future.

I knew a young mother who kept a scrapbook of everything that happened in her first child's life. There were sonogram pictures, gift cards from baby showers, and handwritten notes timing her labor pains. There were literally dozens of pictures of each phase of her little son's growth and development.

Then an unthinkable accident happened. The promising life was ended when the little boy died as the result of an allergic reaction. The mother was already pregnant with a second child, but joy and expectation were taken from her.

I met the mother when that second baby, a little girl, was a toddler. The mother was struggling with issues of grief from the death of her son and overwhelmed with guilt about the stagnant life she was living with her daughter. As she told her story, she talked of her sense of not doing right with this little girl because she was not keeping any mementoes of her life.

"Why?" I asked.

She replied, "I kept such a careful record of my son that perhaps God knew I would have enough things to keep his memory strong, and it would be all right for him to take my son from me. I will not keep a record of my daughter so that God does not claim her, too."

When the words were spoken, the young mother heard the improbability of her "magical thinking." She had kept this protective thought secret to ensure life for her daughter. Telling her secret was a major step in resolving her grief and becoming engaged in life again.

This mother began to experience the connection between the two parts of herself that had been disconnected—the past with her son and the future with her daughter. It was almost a visual event as her words slipped the keystone into place, joining her past to her present and her hope for the future.

In grief, as we enter this phase of Industry versus Inferiority, inferiority often holds the greater power. During this period we struggle with those elements that we have endowed with strength and control through our magical thinking. In this stage of childhood we believe that improvised charms and practices can protect us from this enemy we call death. Tom Sawyer and Huck Finn had incantations and rituals they performed to give them safety in a graveyard at night. It often takes a confrontation or a crisis to create the impetus needed to move beyond this devised protection.

This phase of grief is a time to unlearn old patterns and perhaps learn new ones. The old patterns are those protective ways we created in the throes of our distress. Before old behavior can truly be "unlearned," a new behavior must be ready to take its place. This "new" behavior may indeed be new, but it may simply require us to relearn a way of behaving that served us well before our time of grief. While adopting this new behavior, we come to terms with this aggressor called death so we can begin to experience life to the fullest again. It is an industrious undertaking.

Although it may seem strange, I think the process of cultivating creativity is a needed component in healing grief. I first became aware of the power of creativity from a woman who had been anticipating the birth of her first grandchild. She had been making a quilt for this expected baby, but the baby died before birth. In her sorrow, she put the quilt aside. Months later she made the statement that she felt as incomplete as the baby's quilt. She decided to get the quilt out and finish it. As she worked to create something of beauty, she felt herself becoming whole again.

Being creative can take many forms. It may be learning something entirely new. It may be exploring a latent talent or a secret desire. Or it may be as simple as picking up an old activity. Engaging in creative endeavors allows us to express our feelings in helpful, rather than hurtful, activities. Our creativity may express itself through music, poetry, journaling, painting, sculpting, sewing, cooking; the possibilities are almost endless. It may be quiet work or physical activity like building fences, planting gardens, or digging wells. Primarily it helps us use Industry to conquer Inferiority.

Kevin was creative in gaining a sense of security through writing his needed telephone numbers. The guilt-ridden young mother relearned an old activity and created a scrapbook for her growing daughter. These two grief-stricken people found themselves stronger and more secure as they created their bridges to the present to hold their pasts and futures in place.

QUESTIONS

1. What "numbers" do you need to write so that you, like Kevin, will know you are secure?

2. What steps can you take to put the keystone in place as you reconstruct your sense of security?

3. Make two lists:
    remembered connections with a loved one;
    imagined uncertainties without a loved one.

4. Read your two lists aloud and begin to journal about the old behavior it is now safe to "unlearn" so it can be replaced with new behavior.

5. What creative form may this new step take?

CHAPTER SEVEN

"This makes me remember my babies..."

Grief Recycled

Kevin's world once again had structure, and he felt secure in it. Frequent phone calls and a visit from Granddad and Grandmother had assured him we were still an active part of his life. He was friendly and outgoing with a great love for life in all its forms—not just people but plants, birds, animals, insects, fish, and reptiles. He enjoyed visiting with neighbors and found as much delight in talking with adults as in playing with children. Taylor, his best friend, had a little sister, Leah, who was the age Allison would have been. Kevin had a tenderness with Leah that was poignant to witness. And there was the good news that a new baby was expected in January. Kevin was four years old, full of confidence, and he was going to be a big brother.

Kevin had memories of Allison, and he knew the story of T. J. From the time Kevin was a baby, pictures of T. J. were a part of the familiar things in his house.

As Kevin had grown, so had his knowledge about this brother who was born before him, from the basic fact that T. J. was his brother to the reality that T. J. had died before Kevin had been born. Kevin knew T. J. had never been healthy, that he had spent much of his short life in the hospital, and had died just a few months after his first birthday. Kevin knew he had a brother and a sister, but he had never seen either of them. Now things would be different.

The day after Thanksgiving our phone rang in the middle of the night. Becky's voice was shaky as she said, "I don't want to upset you, but we need your prayers. I'm bleeding heavily and waiting for the ambulance to come. I think I hear it now."

It was several hours before we received the reassuring call from Tom saying that Becky was stable, the baby's heartbeat was strong, and Becky would spend the rest of her pregnancy in the hospital. Once again life changed drastically for Kevin.

Fortunately the hospital did not place restrictions on Kevin's visits to his mom. It was a lot for a four-year-old to absorb, but Kevin seemed to take it in stride. He developed an amazing sense of direction, not only for getting around in a big hospital, but in knowing all the possible routes to take on the thirty-minute drive between his real home and his hospital home. It was as though he was working hard to gain a sense of control over this new experience in his world.

This latest family crisis made me aware it was time to join my husband Ronnie in retirement. It took several days to make this a reality, but by early December we were in Virginia.

Katie was born on December 12. Kevin had gone to preschool that morning knowing that Granddad waited at home for him while his Dad and I were with his Mom at the hospital. By late afternoon Katie's grasp on life was secure enough for Granddad to tell Kevin he had a sister, and it was time for them to go to see her. Kevin was full of excitement.

When Ronnie and Kevin drove into the hospital's parking lot, Ronnie saw Kevin's image in the rearview mirror and was caught off guard by the pale, stricken expression on Kevin's face. Stopping the car, Ronnie turned to Kevin and said, "Kevin, aren't you excited? You're going to see your little sister."

Kevin responded, "This makes me remember my babies who died."

Grief can be re-triggered in the midst of joyous events. It can be anticipated so that we plan and hope we will not be caught off guard at holiday times or by a birthday or anniversary celebration. These grief triggers can be unexpected and innocent, such as the pleasant aroma of freshly brewed coffee on a bright, sunny morning that suddenly brings back the memory of how much a loved one enjoyed that first cup of the day. Through repeated experiences, we may have learned that music can renew an awareness of our loss, but be caught off guard when a movie has that same power. And grief can blind-side us when we experience a happy ending to a tense, traumatic event.

Whatever the trigger, grief can be recycled. We may be filled with dismay or caught by surprise, but suddenly it appears again—this sense of grief, the memory of loss.

Often people ask, "How long does it take?" referring to this recovery period that follows their baptism by grief. I always answer, "It takes as long as it takes." No one can create a timeline for this cycle; each grief is unique and individual. It is determined by who we are, where we are in our journey through life, our past history of events and losses, our emotional and physical health, our social support system, and, most especially, our relationship to the one who died.

In our head we may absorb the knowledge that it will probably take at least a year to work through our grief. This does not mean that we will be in the throes of deep grief for a whole year, but it does mean that we must go through all the events that normally happen in the course of a year. Until we experience the holidays, birthdays, anniversaries, and other celebrations at least once without our loved one, we do not gain a full sense of all that it means to no longer have this person in our midst.

There may be an extended period of time or enough good days in that first year that we feel assured we have conquered this thing called grief; then some anticipated or unexpected event occurs, our grief returns, and we feel we must start all over again.

I've heard this lament so often. "I thought I was doing so well, but I was wrong." The truth is that you were doing well and you were right to say so, but grief is a roller coaster ride of emotions punctuated by highs and lows with times of calm before the next ascent or plunge. We all know that it is not wise to step off the ride before the end.

Our initial reaction to this retriggered grief may be the desire to turn our back, to close down our feelings, and to walk away from the roller coaster of emotion. It is in continuing the journey that we take the next steps in putting ourselves back together.

Erikson says that Fidelity is the quality that evolves in our struggle of Identity versus Role Confusion. Fidelity is faithfulness, loyalty, adherence to promises and duties.

Fidelity is not a word we usually use in talking about grief, but the perception of broken fidelity is often very much present. It may be in the form of unspoken or unacknowledged anger toward our loved one for dying and thereby breaking that bond of loyalty or promise to always be there for us. It may be false guilt placed upon ourself for not being able to perform the duties that our role in life required, for not being faithful in our care. It does not matter where the root of blame rests, broken fidelity is a grief issue, a struggle that is not often explored. It is the basis of our struggle to recreate our role in life and restore our sense of identity.

Whether we are in an initial cycle through grief or suddenly plunged into yet another recycling of this experience of loss, the underlying question once again becomes: "Who am I now without my loved one?"

It had been more than a year since my father died when Mother flew from Georgia to California to visit us. It was her first time to make this trip without Daddy beside her. When we greeted her at the airport, she was full of smiles and generous with her hugs.

That first night we sat up late talking excitedly about family "back home" and the things we would do while she was here. We were all proud of her aura of independence and the way she had put her life back together. Mother was strong.

None of us were prepared for the sudden change the next morning when she stepped into the kitchen, fully dressed and ready for a new day as was her lifelong custom, then collapsed into tears at the smell of the coffee.

Her grief was suddenly fresh and raw again. Being in a different environment, facing another reality of life without the man who had been her husband for more than thirty-five years had brought it back. Although Mother quickly overcame her tears and put a smile back on her face, she was apprehensive throughout the day.

In the afternoon she offered to cook dinner while I was involved in the activities of our then-school-aged children. That night as she was getting ready for bed she said, "Well, I did something today," and we both knew she was referring to more than just frying chicken. She had touched on a new role in life, had added a new dimension to her sense of identity, and experienced a strengthening of the bond of fidelity.

Even though Erikson places ages on his first developmental stages, I think that when we encounter these stages in our growth through grief, there is an agelessness to these struggles. Four-year-old Kevin did not have a vocabulary that included words like fidelity or role confusion. Identity, though, was a word he knew. He could give all the right answers when asked his name, his address, and his phone number. He had learned who he was in his family setting. He was a son to his parents and a grandson to his parents' parents. He was a cousin to some and a nephew to others. And he was a brother, but that defining role in his identity had been swallowed up in stories and memories of loss rather than real-life experiences. Now he took on a new identity as a brother, and his mixed emotions overwhelmed him.

When grief catches us by surprise, we need to be able to spend some time with it. We need to allow it to happen before embarking in a new direction. Granddad sat in the car with Kevin and acknowledged that he, too, remembered T. J. and Allison, and those thoughts made him sad. With the remarkable resiliency of childhood, Kevin, full of smiles and love, was soon ready to greet his new sister.

In the intensity of our struggle through grief, fear of love may be an unacknowledged or unspoken element. We loved another, but death claimed that special person. Now, knowing the pain involved, we fear a repeat of the experience. If, in an attempt to protect ourselves, we shut the door to love, we close the door to positive connections with others. That shut door bars the opportunity to find our new role in life, to establish our new identity, and to create a new sense of fidelity.

There are some who choose to close the door. Whether consciously or unconsciously made, the choice for some is to continue through life as a grief-filled person. It is a path that leads to dependency and ultimately isolation because it says "no" to the possibility of experiencing life in its fullest. It prohibits the next step in Erikson's stages: Intimacy versus Isolation. The choice has been made to not give one's self to others, to not risk love again.

This may well be the crucial point in our journey through grief. The struggle to establish who we are now determines whether we continue to grow or whether we revert once again through Erikson's stages losing our newly found sense of competence and purpose to become a mistrustful person without hope.

Katie was able to leave the hospital in time to be home for Christmas. Despite our apprehension about her need to be on an apnea monitor, it was a jubilant time. We were all caught up in the activities involved with adapting and adjusting to a new baby in the family. In the midst of rejoicing over a crisis happily resolved and the traditions of celebrating this holiday, we began to establish new routines for daily life.

The routine that started each day was Tom, Kevin, and Katie coming downstairs each morning so Katie could be in the midst of family activities under watchful eyes and alert ears. Tom carried Katie while Kevin proudly carried the apnea monitor that was attached to her. Kevin's smile proclaimed his delight in this new identity as protective big brother and told us all that he was accepting the risk to love his little sister.

QUESTIONS

1. Have you, like Kevin, been caught off guard by a resurgence of grief in the midst of what was supposed to be a happy time?

2. Did you turn your back on this retriggered grief?
   Did you allow the grief to override the moment of delight?
   Did you acknowledge what was happening so you could embrace the fullness of yourself?

3. If you could live through that moment again, what, if anything, would you do differently?

CHAPTER EIGHT

"I've got my umbrella in case it rains."

Anticipatory Grief: Preparation for Letting Go

On that Thanksgiving Day before Katie's birth, Becky had called her grandmother. During their conversation she said, "Tom and I have decided that if this baby is a girl, we will name her for you." Mother was thrilled. Not only was this a great compliment to her; the news had come at a low point in her life. Her health was rapidly deteriorating, and we were concerned that the time was fast approaching when she could no longer live independently. Over the next few weeks as we waited in anticipation for Katie's birth, we watched in apprehension as Mother's life began to ebb.

After Katie's premature birth in early December, my oldest brother began to make plans to bring Mother to Virginia so she would have an opportunity to hold her namesake. By Christmas we all acknowledged this was not going to be feasible. Soon after the New Year began, my brother moved Mother into his home and made arrangements for round-the-clock care for her. I made several trips to Georgia to have time with Mother. Tom and Becky searched for ways to make the trip from Virginia so Great-Granny could meet Katie.

In early March Katie was thriving and Tom was able to take a few vacation days. He, Becky, Kevin, and Katie, protected by her apnea monitor, began the five-hundred-mile drive to Augusta, Georgia.

They set out on one of those early spring days that are so spectacular in the South. The extended forecast for the entire southeast was clear skies, mild breezes, and above-normal temperatures. My youngest brother and his wife had come from North Carolina, Ronnie and I flew from California, and we were all with Mother awaiting Katie's arrival.

When the doorbell rang, I hurried to answer it. I opened the door and was almost blinded by the intensity of the afternoon sun. There stood Kevin, full of smiles, waving his hand for me to see what he held as he explained, "I've brought my umbrella in case it rains."

In a time of uncertainty, we all want a safety net. Kevin knew the importance of this long trip. He loved to travel, and he enjoyed being able to introduce his little sister to others. He understood the significance of Katie's name and how eager Great-Granny was to see all of them. And he knew Great-Granny was very sick and would not live much longer. Death and grief were not strangers to him, so he felt a need to be prepared.

What better preparation for an unpredictable spring day than a favorite Mickey Mouse umbrella?

We struggle with and protest against the inevitable when we know death will soon claim a loved one. We go in and out of the now familiar-to-most-of-us phases of anticipatory grief as identified by Elizabeth Kubler-Ross. We attempt to **deny** the reality of what is happening, express our **anger** at the unfairness of it all, **bargain** in an attempt to gain control over the inevitable, succumb to **depression** in the face of our inabilities to change the course of events, and hopefully arrive at that moment of **acceptance** of all that it means.

Even though we often utilize Kubler-Ross's stages of grief after the death of a loved one, her work was primarily with individuals facing the reality of their own impending deaths. Her explanations and definitions apply equally to anyone anticipating the death of a loved one.

Denial is the stage that most readily receives a negative connotation; however, initial denial is often a healthy thing. It is that temporary aura of self-protection that buys time to absorb and helps us begin to deal with an overwhelming new reality. Denial becomes maladaptive when it prevents one from receiving the medical care or emotional support needed to make sense of what is happening.

Denial is the time that can be equated with being an infant who needs the soothing protection of being held tenderly and securely. It is a time that cries out for a comforting lap while an attempt is made to deal with questions of trust and mistrust. Is this news believable, or is it an untruth? Can I trust my ability to deal with it, or will I be incapacitated?

I remember the confusing experience of being a little girl at my grandmother's house when an elderly relative was visiting. Grandmother stood behind me, gently pushing me into the living room with the instructions, "Go sit on Cousin Beulah's lap, and give her a kiss." I was terrified. Cousin Beulah was a woman of great girth. When she sat down, she had no lap. I did not know what to do because I could not understand how to obey Grandmother's instructions.

There are times when we have a sincere desire to support a loved one, but if we lack understanding of what is expected, we cannot follow through. We may give the impression of being so puffed-up, so inflated, with good intentions that we offer no opportunity, no lap, for comfort.

Anger is that defiant expression of the toddler or preschooler who firmly says, "No." When that negative response does not bring a positive result, there is a sense of guilt or shame for our inability to control what is happening.

Bargaining is devising industrious ways to remain in control so that our identity as a person with power and influence is maintained.

Depression isolates us into a state of self-absorption until once again there is enough stability to be open to others.

Acceptance is the surrender moment of replacing despair with inner wisdom; it is the awareness that it does not take physical wholeness to be a person of integrity and purpose.

All too often we may have a basic knowledge of Kubler-Ross's work without a corresponding understanding of it. In our desire to support a loved one, we may strive to hurry that person through the outlined steps so he or she can quickly reach a healing sense of acceptance.

We need to be aware that each person is a unique individual and cannot be programmed or compartmentalized to fit neat definitions. As individuals, each of us must find our own way through the steps. This may mean leapfrogging over one stage and then perhaps backtracking over others. We may jump straight from anger to depression and then fall back into denial before beginning to bargain—or we may just omit a step entirely. Often we cycle through the stages several times before reaching that transforming place of acceptance.

Attempts to hurry another through the stages of grief can often lead to manipulation, trying to force another into a perfect fit. We are people, though, not objects. We need to be supported and encouraged rather than forced and molded.

Anticipatory grief, I think, can cause one to regress in Erikson's stages just as thoroughly as grief in response to an actual loss. This regression can become an opportunity for growth during the ensuing struggle to become whole again.

Many times in an effort to be supportive, we feel we must attach a positive or negative quality to Kubler-Ross's stages. Often the tendency is to label denial a bad thing, thereby proclaiming a need to put it behind and move forward. Like Erikson's competing characteristics of each developmental stage, there are no positive or negative stages in Kubler-Ross's work, but there may be adaptations that should be explored.

It was a family-filled room when Mother saw Katie for the first time. Becky placed Katie in Great-Granny's arms, and time seemed to stand still. Matriarch and infant looked intently into each others eyes, and the smile that radiated from Mother's face gave us all a sense of peace and release. My youngest brother later said it was as though Mother was pouring a lifetime of love into Katie.

That moment of transferring love marked the beginning of letting go for Mother. Only a few months earlier she had **denied** that anything was wrong, even as we became aware of her increasing limitations and declining weight. She had voiced **anger** as she protested moving from her own home, had **bargained** for more time as she procrastinated over the inevitable need for care, and then had shown signs of **depression** as she stopped talking about her former home and the good health and independence she had enjoyed. Now her **acceptance** became so evident it was almost tangible.

Mother's children and grandchildren each dealt with these stages in their own ways. We experienced times of isolation and times when we were able to be together, openly sharing our awareness of what was happening with each other. It was Mother's great-grandchildren who showed the underlying intensity of what we were all experiencing by their actions.

My brother's grandchildren had come to meet Katie and see Kevin and his parents. Jessica and Megan entered the house with uncharacteristic quietness. They remained subdued for a brief period until an adult suggested they might like to go into the backyard to play hide-and-seek. With loud shouts of agreement, the three cousins ran eagerly out the door. It was still a sunny day, but without saying a word, Kevin darted back inside, grabbed his umbrella, ran out again to prop it against the swing set, and with enthusiasm entered the game.

We all need a protective umbrella as we venture into new ways of recreating ourselves. Kevin's symbolic protection was his very tangible umbrella. Mother's protection came through her awareness she would be remembered in the ongoing life of her family and through a renewed sense of integrity as our mother, grandmother, and great-grandmother. Her umbrella was a little girl whose life assured Mother her love would continue to be a part of ours.

QUESTIONS

1. What are the things that upset you?
   How do you deal with them?

2. Kevin carried an umbrella on a sunny day as he faced an emotionally charged time. Can you describe your "umbrella" (your own safety net) that you keep handy for an unpredictable experience?

CHAPTER NINE

"Where is my old house?
Did it just go away?"

Moving On

During the summer before Kevin was two years old, Tom and Becky made plans to sell their home in Escondido. Kevin knew a loved and protected life there with neighbors who openly showed him much attention. Sitting around the dinner table one evening, they talked of moving to a new house. With sudden understanding, Kevin began to voice an awareness of potential loss as he named his neighbors asking, "No more Barbara?" and then, "No more Thomas and Emily?" Barbara was an across-the-street neighbor who was like an extra grandmother in his life, and Thomas and Emily were his playmates. At an early age he began to learn that losses occur when we move on to something new.

We encounter losses all through life. At the moment of birth we experience the loss of the womb's security as we are thrust into an alien world that is overwhelmingly large and different from our first environment. Some losses may be insignificant, and some may seem insurmountable. The loss of a pacifier to an infant who takes only occasional interest in it is far different from that same loss to the baby who constantly holds it in his mouth.

Whether the losses are unremarkable or overwhelming is not crucial. The crucial factors are our own perception of the loss and whether we are allowed to express our hurt and disappointment in a supportive and compassionate environment. As we grow and mature, our ability to handle losses as adults is built upon a foundation rooted in early childhood. It is our preparation for those ultimate losses that inevitably come into our life—the loss of someone near and dear to us.

When Kevin and his parents moved to the new house in Oceanside, they had new experiences and new neighbors. There was a time of adjustment when everything was different and no one was familiar, but very quickly three-year-old Samantha became Kevin's almost constant companion. Barbara from the old neighborhood might come to visit and tell stories about Thomas and Emily, but if Samantha rang the doorbell there would be shrieks of excitement as though she and Kevin had been separated for weeks rather than a few hours.

Kevin adapted to the loss of his old house and was moving on with his life. Then, a few months after the move from Escondido to Oceanside, Kevin broke a silent time in the car with the question: "Where is my old house? Did it just go away?"

Life continues, but we do not forget. It may be a thought that comes to mind or an event that occurs, but something triggers a memory and we begin to wonder. For Kevin at age two-and-a-half, his wondering had to do with the physical location of his old house because it was no longer in his day-to-day life. As adults after the death of a loved one, the wondering may be more in the form of a life review. It might encompass the "what-ifs" had this death not happened or the course we must take to deal with the realities of our new lives. In any event this wondering marks the reality of moving on—of life continuing even though there has been a change.

I once knew a remarkable gentleman who told of three blessings that had come into his life in a short period of time: he became a grandfather, was diagnosed with heart disease, and then discovered he had prostate cancer. In reflecting back on that year, he would say that people needed no explanation to understand the first blessing—becoming a grandfather. But the blessings he found in his two life-threatening diseases were not readily perceived. His own understanding had come in retrospect, after struggling through not only the rigors of medical intervention but also in resolving his thoughts and feelings in his search for a cure. In the process he learned the difference between "cure" and "healing." His thesis was that people seek a "cure," meaning they want life to be the way it was before something went wrong. "Healing" means life has forever changed, there is no going back to what used to be. It allows one's life to be transformed and become more than what it was before. One may be sick, broken, and limited, yet better.

This gentleman experienced that acceptance time we work toward in anticipatory grief and that "moving on" time in life-review moments, when we realize our life has been irrefutably changed by our journey through grief. It is the time we come to realize the truth in the analogy of the bare root tree—that "bare roots bear fruit" and we have become productive again.

These life-review moments may come unannounced in quiet, reflective moments; they may be intentional times when we assess change in our pattern of living; they may be muddled, unrecognized mental quandaries during developmental stages; or they may be a sense of foreboding or fear in the midst of yet another crisis. However they present themselves, these review moments are launching pads for moving on with life. Most often we initially fail to see them as stepping stones to the future but rather view them as stumbling blocks in our journey through grief.

I remember one early morning when I was home alone a few months after Allison's death. I was not doing anything, just sitting quietly, looking out the window and thinking of how my life had changed. Among other things, I was very much aware my prayer life had become a rote routine and my faith felt flat. The air had a chill to it, the skies were dark with clouds that threatened rain, but the almond tree in our backyard was beautiful. As I focused on it, I became aware of the seeming incongruity of a wintry day and a blooming almond tree. The atmosphere was foreboding, but there was an essence of hope in the white blossoms.

That morning I became aware that if Allison's life was to have a positive and lasting effect on me, I needed to change. I could not return to the way life was when we all anticipated her birth. Kevin had said, "My baby died, but I still love her." I began to realize that my love for Allison would always be present, for she had become a permanent part of my memory and who I am today. I felt as though I was on the threshold of a new awareness of life's fullness. I was still struggling, but I was beginning to feel like our almond tree with blossoms of promise in the midst of winter. A reflective life review does not mean all is immediately resolved, but it becomes a pivotal moment in the healing process.

I also have memories of numerous women who came to me for counseling as they struggled with the realities of widowhood. Quite often after months or years grieving a husband's death, one might return with a new issue—remarriage—framed in a sense of loss over a name change. The newly found sense of identity and wholeness was threatened by the perceived new identity that would result from taking the name of a new husband. This issue was the catalyst to assess strengths and weaknesses, memories of the past, and hopes for the future. It was the opportunity to evaluate growth through grief and acknowledge the positive qualities acquired through that growth. Contemplating a new marriage caused a definitive life-review moment, an intentional assessment period to evaluate a change in a pattern of living.

Not all life-review moments are as easily defined or recognized. Those that come simultaneously with developmental changes or as a result of a new crisis are often hidden in the struggles of the moment.

Developmentally Kevin grew in leaps and bounds, mentally, physically, emotionally, and socially. He readily accepted extra credit assignments in school and excelled with them. His clothes were outgrown before the shine of newness disappeared. Over time he helped tell Katie the stories of T. J. and Allison, and together they learned about little Dustin, their brother who was stillborn, too tiny to survive when Kevin was still a toddler.

Kevin celebrated his twelfth birthday and began a new school year well aware it would be his last year in elementary school. Even though it was only September, he was already anticipating middle school the next year. Then September 11 happened.

Despite the fact Kevin had shown remarkable growth in many ways over the years, he still struggled with what seemed to be a lifelong inability to fall asleep easily. Through the years an easy explanation of this pattern had emerged. The first night that newborn

Kevin was home from the hospital, Tom had begun the routine of reading a nighttime story to him. Initially this story time was in the rocking chair with Kevin cradled in his dad's arm. When Kevin outgrew his crib and moved into a "big boy" bed, this special activity moved to Kevin's room with Tom lying beside him while reading the nightly story. As Kevin grew bigger and learned to read, the routine continued with Tom bringing a chair into Kevin's room and sitting beside his bed as they both enjoyed this reading time together.

Often, though, sleep did not come readily when the latest chapter ended. There were frequent times when Kevin appeared in the family room long after his light was turned out with the plaintive phrase, "I can't go to sleep." It did not seem too great a problem until Kevin began to struggle with invitations for sleepovers at friends' houses or a Boy Scout camping trip. His inability to go to sleep readily became an obstacle to having fun away from home.

After September 11 the oft-repeated phrase, "you'll outgrow this" began to lose its encouraging tone. His difficulty going to sleep increased, and Kevin's sleep was often interrupted with sad dreams that disturbed him.

It was easy to find reasons behind the increasing sleep problems. Kevin's home in Virginia was near Washington, D.C., and neighbors had jobs at the Pentagon or with the CIA, FBI, Secret Service, and airlines flying from nearby Dulles Airport. Two neighborhood boys had been with their parents in the hotel connected to the World Trade Towers and had run for five miles to flee the inferno. The father of one of the scouts in Kevin's troop had been on one of the doomed planes.

When Ronnie and I flew to Virginia for Christmas, I readily agreed with everyone that Kevin's increased nighttime apprehension was very understandable. My concern increased though when a few days before our scheduled flight home, Kevin became tearful and sad as evening approached. On our last night in Virginia he voiced concerns about our safety in flying home and told us over and over he wished we all could live together.

I came home with a heavy heart. I knew that Kevin was in a major developmental stage of his life, and the counselor in me recognized that these stages are also times when grief is recycled. Parents who live through the death of a child will revisit their grief at each major stage or life event that child would have known—what would have been the first day of school, graduation, or a possible marriage. These potential events are experienced in the context of things that will not be, and they are mourned. In the same manner, young children review their grief experiences at each developmental stage as they become aware of what this past loss means to them now.

Kevin was struggling with not just a foreboding that seemed to grip our entire nation; he was also dealing with his need to understand the grief he had experienced so early in life in the context of his growing maturity. His complaints of not being able to sleep were followed by admissions of being sad that T. J., Dustin, and Allison had died. He began to say things, such as "Why did T. J. and Dustin have to die? I always wanted to have a brother."

Life review may be a brief interlude that opens the way for a new direction, but most often life review transpires over a greater period of time. It may be a few days, or it may be a long, drawn-out process. It is another necessary step in growing through grief. In fact, it is an essential step needed so we can move on with life.

It was only in working on this book that I realized the true depth of all that Kevin had been experiencing in his nightly struggles to go to sleep. I found a letter I had written to my mother soon after Allison's death telling her of Kevin's procrastination at bedtime and how one night he had voiced the fear, "If I go to sleep, I may die."

We can't escape our pasts. Our past issues of loss and major crises are part and parcel of who we are today, but that does not have to mean they are a detrimental part of our present. It is in working through these events, mourning our losses, and entertaining our life reviews that we reach the place of acceptance experienced by my remarkable gentleman friend who could count what might be considered tragic diagnoses as eventual blessings.

Kevin had learned over the years that it was safe to voice his thoughts and feelings because he had supportive and understanding parents who were able to listen. Still it was a prolonged process with ups and downs. After September 11 there were unsuccessful and then successful attempts to stay overnight with friends.

Summer 2002 arrived, and Kevin left on a camping trip with apprehension. He came home elated over his wonderful adventures and experiences. Ronnie and I made another visit to Virginia, and Kevin saw us off with a smile while still expressing the desire that we lived closer.

In September 2003 Kevin was adjusting to middle school, increased responsibilities, and a new crisis. One evening when I called, Kevin answered the phone and proudly told me that his parents were out and he was the one responsible for Katie. When I asked him about school, he said, "It's pretty good, except for being on Code Blue." Kevin and Katie lived in the area of Virginia being terrorized by the then-unknown sniper. Their schools now operated in "lock-down" mode that kept the students inside throughout the day.

A few days later I talked to Becky and learned that both Kevin and Katie were pleased to be trusted to be home without a sitter when Mom and Dad went to their Bible study class. The ground rules were simple: they were to be considerate to each other, Katie was to be in bed by eight o'clock, and Kevin's bedtime was no later than 8:30. Best of all, when Tom and Becky returned home at nine o'clock, Katie and Kevin were both asleep.

Like the old house in Escondido, Kevin's experiences of loss did not "just go away," but he had moved on.

QUESTIONS

1. In your grief, have you had a glimpse of "blossoms of promise?"

    If so, journal about your insight into ways you are beginning to experience the truth that "bare roots bear fruit."

    If not, begin to list the ways in which the life of your loved one has enabled you to become a better person.

2. As you journal, remember that a reflective life review does not mean all is immediately resolved, but it is a pivotal moment in the healing process.

CHAPTER TEN

"I didn't really know her."

Epilogue

In the winter months following September 11, an additional crisis entered Kevin's life. Grandma Bellino, his paternal grandmother, was in the terminal phase of an eight-year struggle with Alzheimer's disease. At the height of Kevin's time of increased anxiety, sadness, and sleep problems, Tom flew to California to see his mother and visit his brother and sisters.

After a few days Grandma Bellino's physical condition stabilized enough for Tom to return to Virginia. Amid numerous questions and concerns from Kevin, Tom and Becky wondered what should be done when his mother died. Would it be best to have Becky remain home with Kevin and Katie so there would be less disruption in their routines, or to go as a family for her funeral so there would be fewer unknowns in their lives?

Just a few days before school spring break and before these uncertainties were resolved, Grandma Bellino died. Suddenly the decision seemed easy—they would all go.

We might anticipate an event with great trepidation, thinking the easier course would be to avoid or even ignore the situation or at least minimize the involvement. It might be another grief in our life, or it might be the reality of an approaching holiday or celebration while we still feel incomplete in our aloneness. Even when we realize we must face the unavoidable, as protective adults we still want to shield our children from the hard lessons of life. Unknowns usually prove to be more fearful than the actual experience. All of us, adults as well as children, cope better with difficult situations if we have a sense of structure, a plan to serve as a guide. Most often the outcome proves our inner strength.

Kevin and Katie were told that Grandma Bellino had died and they would all fly to California for her funeral. Then Tom and Becky told Kevin his uncle and aunts wanted him to join his five adult cousins serving as pallbearers for their grandma. He accepted the honor and responsibility with poise, but then said, "I didn't really know her."

Both Kevin and Katie knew their dad's mother. There were pictures of each of them being held by her when they were infants. Kevin's memory did not retain the time he was very young and she was still healthy. His memories of Grandma Bellino were the same as

Katie's—being with her when they made infrequent trips to California. They knew her as the grandma who lived with Aunt Suzie and liked to play dolls with their cousin Chelsea. They remembered her big smile and even bigger hugs, the way she would hold them tightly and sway gently during a long embrace. They had memories of the way she liked to watch them play and how she tried to toss or catch a ball with them. They did not have memories of being able to have conversations with her—of sharing stories and experiences and getting to know her. Now Kevin realized he did not know just who this grandmother was.

It was Granddad's idea. With Tom and Becky's approval, he asked Kevin if he would like to make a documentary of Grandma Bellino's life. At the reception following the funeral, Kevin used Granddad's video camera to interview family and friends, asking them to tell him a special memory about his Grandma Bellino. He recorded stories from her sister, her deceased husband's brother, her children and grandchildren, and her neighbors and close friends. Each told of some way in which they had known her specialness.

Erikson stated that his theory holds true in all societies and cultures. During the elementary school stage, young people learn the basic skills of society. In primitive cultures the young might learn to herd cattle, till the soil, gather food, or weave. In more advanced cultures these lessons embrace academic skills, and in our society today, computer literacy.

In the next several days Kevin proved the competency he had gained during this stage as he scanned a collection of family pictures portraying Grandma Bellino's life, edited them into his videotape, created graphics and credits, recorded background music, and reproduced copies of his creation for family members.

Even though Erikson assigns parameters of age to his early stages of development, I think that trauma erases these age boundaries. Regardless of our age at the time of our grief-induced regression to childlike ways of being, there is an agelessness in our return to integrity as we heal. The developmental stages may progress out of order without any attachment to chronological age. I also think that children who work their way back to a sense of wholeness can develop a maturity that goes beyond Erikson's age and stage constraints.

When I first began my counseling career, the hospital where I worked had a hospice component. Through my work there I met a young boy who had lived with cystic fibrosis all his life. During one of his many hospitalizations, he celebrated his tenth birthday. The nurses decorated his room with banners and helium balloons. The kitchen baked a birthday cake and supplied ice cream. Secretaries, receptionists, and technicians came to celebrate with him. The most memorable part of that day for me was seeing doctors come, sit at this boy's bedside in a relaxed manner, and have cheerfully funny, philosophical conversations with him. He was only ten, but his acceptance of a lifelong medical trauma had launched him into a maturity far beyond his age. He knew who he was and the limits of his life. His respect and concern for others provided the platform that displayed the wisdom gained in what Erikson would call the struggle of Integrity versus Despair. He was young, frail, and broken, but psychologically and spiritually he was whole.

*   *   *

At the end of the week his family spent in California, Kevin returned to Virginia feeling he now had come to know his Grandma Bellino. His creative endeavor to document her life gave him a feeling of wholeness and brought him into a closer bond with his extended family. Standing on the brink of his teen years in what Erikson labels Identity versus Role Confusion, Kevin developed a maturity rooted in the wisdom gained from his accumulated experiences. He knows he is a survivor.

As Kevin began producing his documentary, other family members became involved in the process. Some contributed pictures, some searched for recordings of their mother's favorite songs, and some had insights into lessons they thought their mother would want her grandchildren to know. They all shared an interest in Kevin's project, and this shared interest started a dialogue. They talked and compared memories among themselves and across the generations. Their dialogue began the process of creating the bridge that would connect their pasts with their future.

Often I have thought of a family as being very much like a mobile. Mobiles come in varied sizes and styles, but they all have the common characteristic of being composed of objects suspended by a thin, strong string attached to supporting rods. When they are balanced and in place, they move and sway. Sometimes the slightest breeze can make the objects come into contact with each other, producing a pleasant sound. If a single object is removed from the balanced mobile, it is suddenly in disarray. It takes time and trial and error to bring the tangled mobile back into a functioning balance.

Families struck by death are like that tangled mobile. A member has been taken away, and suddenly everybody and everything is out of balance. It takes time and effort to define new roles and trial and error to reestablish a sense of purpose and place so all can function well again.

My hope is that all of you who read this will be able to write an epilogue to your own story. It would tell of your ability to be creative in not only shaping your future but also finding harmony and balance with your past and accepting your new place and position in your ongoing life.

QUESTIONS

1. If you had a mobile that represented your family before the death of your loved one, how would it look?

2. Sketch, or describe, the model for a mobile that would represent your situation as it now exists.

3. What creative steps can you take to rebalance your mobile?

4. Are you ready to write the epilogue to your own story?

APPENDIX

Erik Erikson is different from most theorists in that his description of personality development covers the entire lifespan, rather than just to the age of adulthood. For the first several stages he defines the age parameters, but after the teen years, he no longer gives demographics for personality growth.

AGE (in years)	STRUGGLE		
0–1	Trust	vs.	Mistrust
1–3	Autonomy	vs.	Shame
3–6	Initiative	vs.	Guilt
6–12	Industry	vs.	Inferiority
12–18	Identity	vs.	Role Confusion
	Intimacy	vs.	Isolation
	Generativity	vs.	Self-Absorption
	Integrity	vs.	Despair

Erikson explains that each age/stage of development is a struggle between two characteristics. He is quick to caution that labels of "positive" or "negative" not be applied to these characteristics, for we need to experience each element of each struggle in our development. He explains that should we not have any times of mistrust in our basic struggle between Trust and Mistrust, we would become a very gullible person. Furthermore, he proposes that out of each developmental stage a quality or strength emerges. For example, from this struggle of Trust versus Mistrust, the emerging quality is Hope. According to Erikson, this hope is the foundation for faith to grow.

In this initial developmental stage, the need is to establish a basic sense that some person or aspect of our environment is dependable. The opposing fear is separation from that sense of dependability—loss of care. As an infant Kevin went through a stage where he would initially cry when his mother left him with a neighbor. It would not take long for Barbara's smiles, hugs, and soothing voice to bring Kevin back to a sense of security. He became aware that he was with someone who cared.

Erikson's stage of Autonomy versus Shame is the time when a toddler seeks independence and freedom—that time frame we call "the terrible twos." It is the stage in which we begin to develop a capacity to reflect, to question and explore, and to think and daydream. It is also the time when attitude is expressed with the simple words "me" and "mine," and the most-used word in the vocabulary is "no." From this struggle the strength that emerges is Will or a sense of determination.

As Kevin approached his second birthday, many of my friends would smile knowingly and say, "Uh-oh! The terrible twos!" I was determined that for Kevin and me at least this period would be different—it would be a delightful year in his life. I would counter my friends' comments and say, "No, the terrific twos." It became a fun-filled time, and it was a time of challenges for Kevin.

There were many occasions during that period when Kevin had to deal with moments of Shame. These were times when he suddenly became aware that he had made a wrong choice, his idea was not working, and his inability was seen by others as well as himself. Kevin was exposed and knew he was exposed; he would turn his back or hide his face and cry.

A foundation is set and growth continues with the next stage: Initiative versus Guilt. This is the play age of life. Play is such a predominant feature of this stage that it often gives rise to the comment that "play is the work of childhood." It is the time not only to play but also to develop courage to pursue a goal. And it is the time when play or pursuit of these goals is often misdirected or unsafe and met with punishment. At this age, punishment is felt as a lack or loss of love. The resulting emotion is Guilt and a sense of being or doing wrong.

This is the stage Kevin was entering when Tom and Becky took him for a tour of the hospital where his new brother or sister would be born. Kevin was excited to be the focus of attention in an adult world, to hear about the care Mom would receive in the hospital, and to see the nursery filled with new babies. Most exciting of all, though, was being able to dress-up in scrubs, to put on a doctor's mask, and then have his picture taken holding a life-size doll. He returned home, talked about, and played out the events that would happen soon. Kevin's involvement in these activities would lead toward this stage's developing quality: Purpose.

The elementary-school-age child is the focus of Erikson's next developmental stage—Industry versus Inferiority. Erikson points out that his theory is universal and holds true even in developing countries where school is not the norm. It is the time to learn the "how-tos," the tasks of society. In third-world countries this might be learning to tend a flock or plow a field. In our country, our children or grandchildren are introduced to skills we could not imagine in our early schooling—they work to master the technology of computers. It is a time to learn not only how-to, but to gain the courage to pursue thoughts and goals. During this period a battle against a sense of Inferiority, which one feels when mistakes are made or progress in learning is slow, begins. This sense of Inferiority makes one feel rejected or inadequate. Through these years Competence is the strength pursued.

I am sure we all have vivid memories of our teen years, the time Erikson identifies as the struggle between Identity and Role Confusion. This is the time when we want to experience life to the fullest extent possible, yet we struggle to discover who we are. Erikson says that identity is the sense of being at one with self as we grow and develop (a respect of self) and a sense of affinity with our community's future as well as its history. Missteps lead to a sense of role confusion, and our answer to the internal question, "who am I?" becomes, "ultimately, I am alone." Peer pressure weighs heavily to keep that sense of being alone at bay. It is a crucial developmental stage for the emerging quality: Fidelity.

Fidelity sets the stage for Erikson's next struggle: Intimacy versus Isolation. He stresses the need to understand his meaning of "Intimacy," saying he is referring to "Intimacy" with an upper case "I." This "upper case Intimacy" is not only a sense of self respect but a capacity to commit or give of self to another, even when it means compromise and sacrifice. This Intimacy is a mature mutuality and is not to be confused with the more self-centered lower case "i" intimacy which is often expressed sexually and can lead to a sense of aloneness or Isolation. Love is the evolving quality of this stage and the cornerstone for the next: Generativity versus Self Absorption.

Once again Erikson stresses the importance of understanding his vocabulary. He says Generativity is a concern with the next generation, but he does not mean we must have children of our own to develop fully through this stage. We need to be interested in the next generation, in the ongoing process of our culture and society, so we are not pulled into an aloneness that is expressed in Self Absorption. Response to this instinctual impulse to cherish and to help enables the development of the quality of Care.

At some undefined moment in our growth we reach that stage of Integrity versus Despair with its emerging strength: Wisdom. Even though it appears as the final stage of Erikson's theory, it is not defined or restricted to a time of "old age." I have worked with young children experiencing life-threatening illnesses who come to this time in their brief lives when, despite their sufferings, they gain a sense of coherence and wholeness expressed in Wisdom far beyond their years. It is that time when we adapt to or accept the place we happen to be. We can look back on our pasts, see the good and the bad, and become aware of the lessons we have learned. In Erikson's words, we become a reservoir of strength, a collector of time, and a preserver of memories.

My hope—my prayer—for each of you is that you grow through your time of grief, adapting to and accepting the place you happen to be. May you see both the positive and the negative in your loss as you become aware of the lessons you have learned. May you realize that you are a better person because your loved one's life touched yours.